The Modern Activist

Masterminded Solutions For Everyday Situations

Anonymous G

Table of Contents

Introduction

Are you an immigrant looking for a quality society in which to settle? Perhaps, you're a refugee looking for a place to start over? Or, you're an asylum-seeker trying to settle with your family and live an honest life? Perhaps, you are an American who is looking to live in an equal society? Or, you are questioning the motives of the current US government, American society and culture, and your place in it? Whichever your situation might be, you're left with many difficult choices. Since the beginning of massive immigration in 2015, the US, Canada, and EU countries have received millions of people.

Many found a safe haven in their preferred country, but experienced a swift turn in the tides with the outcome of the 2016 US elections. The USA used to be a number one destination for refugees, immigrants, and asylum-seekers. It offered many job opportunities, and promised a new, better life to anyone who was looking for a fresh start. However, things have since gone downhill. Trump's administration fired up an anti-immigrant rhetoric, and gave the minority of those against social equality far too much say and power. While it's true that over 70% of white Americans support immigration (Krogstad, 2020) and equal rights for minorities, gross violations of human rights that mainly targeted people of color changed the scenery of US society in 2020.

Protests, demonstrations, and civil unrests have been raging since 2019, despite the risks from Covid-19. In this book, we'll discuss whether US society is as democratic and stable as it once was, and whether it's still the best choice for immigrants. We'll also present you with a long list of other countries who welcome immigrants and refugees so that you know the full scope of your options. Finally, you will learn about which particular things make said societies stand out, but also the problems you could come across when adapting to a new environment.

Chapter 1: The Problem

Has the time when the USA was a haven for all those seeking refuge and looking to start over officially passed? The current political situation in the USA doesn't seem to promote social equality. In fact, 2020 began with protests and demonstrations revolving around racism and unequal treatment of minorities. The most recent events (Mar-Jul 2020) seem to suggest that civil unrest has yet to reach its peak. But, what appears most concerning is that the current US government no longer finds itself accountable for malpractice. In this chapter, we'll review the events that have caused the US, in 2020, to become a potentially unstable environment.

Political Stability in USA

In many ways, the USA is one of the world's leading economic and military forces. Their domestic product accounts for nearly a quarter of the world. It is a country that arose from immigration and has, for a long time, supported those who arrive at its borders looking for a new life. However, Trump's administration seems to have affected that trend negatively.

Despite winning the 2016 election, the current (2020) US president and the political decisions and changes brought on from his government proceed to cause civil unrest. Many claim that the current administration has managed to undo much of the progress brought on by its predecessors (Packer, 2020).

Curbing illegal immigration was one of Trump's three biggest goals, and statistics indicate success so far. Consequently, the brute and unethical practices used for the sake of this goal continue to cause public outrage on a daily basis. This matter is made worse with the notion that having a political party that is often accused of racism and misogyny in power encourages the like-minded to pursue their unethical ways even further.

The Trump administration became a synonym for racism and bigotry. Simultaneously, shocking events continue to shake the US population. Blatant demonstrations of police brutality and disregard for human rights, often geared towards minorities, women, and the LGBTQ community, are becoming public.

Yet, the obvious lack of government initiative to intervene with malpractice and obvious crime being committed by its officials begs the question of whether or not the USA is still safe, or if it is still the best option, for immigrants and refugees.

Treatment of Minorities in USA

Current data shows that the USA may have become less minority-friendly than it once was. Research shows that people of all races and ethnicities are increasingly dissatisfied with the treatment of minorities. The issue seems to be most related to race and ethnicity, and less related to religion and other metrics. Fewer Americans are satisfied with how minorities are being treated in society, with the ratio of satisfied versus dissatisfied ranges between 40% and 50% on each side of the spectrum across white, black, Hispanic, Asian, and Arab communities (Jones, 2019).

Survey participants mainly blamed the rhetoric of Trump's administration, which is considered hostile towards minorities, for the decline in social fairness and equal treatment (Jones, 2019). The year 2018 noted a significant decline in satisfaction with societal treatment compared to 2016.

It's also relevant to know that subjects were asked to voice their (dis)satisfaction pertaining to minority treatment in different situations and settings. The most concerning findings suggest that the majority of unfair treatment happens in healthcare and in contact with the authorities (police treatment). These findings point out that minorities face the biggest struggles while shopping at stores, and while receiving healthcare and assistance from government officials.

Nearly 30% of all subjects perceived that blacks are commonly treated unfairly across a variety of daily situations. Current statistics also indicate that the vast majority of Americans (75%) are supportive of immigration but also are increasingly unhappy with how immigrants and refugees are treated by authorities (Jones, 2019).

Civil Unrest And Police Brutality

After an incident that took place on May 25, when the arrest of George Floyd resulted in his death, a series of police brutality incidents have surfaced, or have gained more attention than they would have in the past. The public outrage that resulted in nation-wide protests was first sparked by the murder of Breonna Taylor that took place on Mar 13, 2020. Taylor was tragically gunned down in her apartment, supposedly by accident, after two armed police officers entered her apartment in a search for two suspected drug dealers.

As of now (Aug 2020), some of the police officers involved in this incident were fired, but no criminal charges were filed. There is, however, a long history of police brutality committed against minorities. The year 2016 was marked by the killing of Philando Castile. Freddie Gray (2015), Tamir Rice (2014), and Michael Brown (2014) were only some of the cases that sparked outrage and raised the issue of police brutality in the USA.

Demonstrations and protests that followed caused concerns over alleged disproportionate use of force by the US police.

Elizabeth Throssell, a spokeswoman for the UN Rights Office, expressed concerns due to arbitrary arrests, as well as the discriminatory and disproportionate use of force by the authorities (UN News, 2020).

As you can see, the political climate in American society has changed significantly since the Obama administration, which was said to have made numerous advancements to the country's immigration policies and minority treatment. This begs the question of whether or not moving to the USA should be your primary goal, or that there are, perhaps, other choices for you?

In the next chapter, we'll review how the US has changed in terms of its social climate and immigration policy. We'll discuss what immigration looks like for the average person, and whether or not there are better alternatives.

Chapter 2: Food for Thought

Is the USA Your Best Choice?

On July 22, 2020, the federal court in Canada ruled that the country's asylum agreement with the US was invalid due to refugee human rights violations. Although the Safe Third Country Agreement (STCA) states that refugees will seek shelter in the first safe country they reach, it no longer applies to the US, due to refugee imprisonment (BBC News, 2020). The judge's ruling proclaimed the deal unconstitutional, in favor of Canadian immigration activists. This ruling essentially means that refugees who were unable to stay in Canada due to the STCA no longer have to fear deportation to the US. This ruling deems the US no longer safe for those who seek asylum.

Many victims have come forward, describing their traumatic experiences while being held in isolation. According to Canada officials, the recent ruling will reduce irregular crossings of the country's borders to avoid being returned to the US.

However, these events are only the culmination of the US government's shift in immigration policies. Claims that the US government exposed asylum-seekers to inhumane treatment, familial separation, and even torture, date back to 2017 and 2018.

Although at that time, the US recorded the lowest number of asylum-seekers in its long history, legal changes have been made to grossly limit access to asylum-seekers. The country is said to have broken international laws by implementing methods like refugee pushbacks, imprisonment, and the removal of children from their families.

These recorded practices, as Canadian authorities rule, were far from unfounded. In fact, the US is now being accused of exposing a large number of asylum-seekers to inhumane living conditions, compromising their safety due to being held up at the Mexican border, and leaving them vulnerable to crime and human trafficking in said conditions. The list of accusations against the US government is long and difficult to comprehend, and the claims that Trump's administration is looking to "dismantle the immigration system" in order to stop asylum-seekers from reaching the US has now been accepted as true by both the US and the Canadian public.

However, there is hope that this situation will be only temporary. As a vast majority of Americans (75%) support immigrants in their efforts to settle in the US, pending elections bring hope. With Democrat and liberal candidates showing a promising reputation among

US residents, many of the pro-human-rights and pro-immigration organizations in the US are working devotedly to help improve the situation for asylum-seekers.

Organizations like Amnesty International, UNICEF USA, National Immigration Forum, National Immigration Law Center, International Rescue Committee, and Migration Policy Institute are only some of the dozens of organizations that advocate for fair reception and humane treatment of immigrants, refugees, and asylum-seekers.

While the upcoming change in immigration policies in the US seems promising with a possible change in political leadership, it is questionable whether it will happen fast enough for those looking for, and needing, immediate help.

Why You Should Find an Alternative Option

Currently, there are many arguments against seeking asylum in the USA. First and foremost, you're technically allowed to seek asylum in Canada, where you're guaranteed much better treatment. Dangers like facing unfair treatment, imprisonment, or a violation of human rights are currently far too real for anyone in question. Regardless of whether or not you believe these claims to be true, you can expect to face long waiting times at US borders, unlawful imprisonment without reasonable cause, isolation, and separation from children and family.

Chapter 3: Countries Who Welcome Refugees

Countries That Welcome Immigrants

Aside from the best-known destinations for refugees, immigrants, and those seeking asylum, the following countries are also known for their pro-immigrant policy (US News, 2020):

- Sweden welcomed 132,000 immigrants in 2017, which was only 15% fewer than it did the previous year. The number of applications is currently dropping, with around 20000 applications being sent yearly. According to the 2016 global survey, Sweden is considered to be the best country for immigrants.
- The Netherlands is also known for accepting a high number of asylum-seekers as permanent immigrants. Those numbers had been rising by 2% yearly until 2016, when a gradual decline in asylum requests was recorded.

- Italy accepted 21,600 immigrants in 2017. Italy has a high level of foreign nationals, with nearly 5,000,000 people coming from Balkans, Asia, and East Europe.
- Australia also received over 200,000 permanent immigrants during 2017 and continues to receive around 30,000 asylum requests yearly. However, conditions in which immigrants are received were condemned by human rights advocates because a small staying fee is required in the states of Papua New Guinea and Nauru. It's also important to note that Australia doesn't receive asylum-seekers who arrive by boat.
- France also receives a high number of immigrants, averaging over 200,000 permanent immigrants yearly since 2015. The country issues over 20,000 work permits yearly on average.
- Canada received near 300,000 immigrants in 2017 and continues its pro-immigrant policies. The country plans to receive around 340,000 immigrants by the end of 2020.
- Spain accepted 324,100 immigrants in 2017 and continues to improve facilities and funding for the accommodation of refugees, immigrants, and asylum-seekers.
- The United Kingdom also received over 300,000 permanent immigrants in 2017, similar to 2016, but its political scene indicates a possible change to discourage further asylum-seekers.
- Germany is one of the most promising destinations for immigrants. The country received over 800,000 immigrants in 2017 alone, and over 700,000 in 2016. The country's admirable immigration, asylum-seeking, and refugee policies make it one of the main desired destinations for migrants due to job opportunities and financial wellbeing.

Highest Equality Societies

Previously mentioned countries rank high in the number of immigrants they accept. However, the list would look different if you were to rank countries by the quality of life they provide. In these terms, Canada assumes the first spot when it comes to welcoming immigrants and providing job opportunities.

Switzerland ranks second, with its neutrality and wealthy status playing a crucial role in how immigrants are being treated. This country has quite low unemployment rates, with urban population making up the majority of its residents. Switzerland didn't take sides in any recent wars or armed conflicts, and has greatly prospered because of this.

Sweden is considered to be one of the most progressive societies in the world. A high level of social equality and low crime rates, compared to great material wealth at the country's disposal, make Sweden one of the prominent destinations for immigrants. Sweden is mainly a capitalist society with advanced transportation networks and infrastructure. The country promotes equal wealth contribution and greatly invests in public service.

Australia is considered to be a wealthy nation, with an economy based on the market, driven by commodities exports and its service sector. The country pays close attention to environmental issues and is committed to reducing greenhouse gas emissions.

Germany is one of Europe's largest economic leaders, with a strong social service and social market economy. Legal immigrants in Germany are granted a wide variety of services, including a full scope of medical care, social workers and therapists that are assigned to help them get used to living in a new environment, language education, and schooling according to one's desires and abilities.

Denmark may not be one of the countries that receives a high number of immigrants, but it is an equal society where you can expect fair, humane treatment. Denmark has a highly advanced healthcare system with mainly free medical care and higher education.

The Netherlands ranks high both in the number of immigrants they receive and the quality of their treatment. The Dutch are considered to be a highly tolerant society, with liberal views on different cultures coexisting, same-sex marriage, drugs, prostitution, and euthanasia.

Finland is a typical Nordic country in many ways. Liberal views, social equality, and low unemployment rates all create a prosperous environment in which to live. High education quality, healthcare, and quality of life are among the country's staple benefits.

Chapter 4: What to Expect

Learning New Languages

Many immigrants who come to Canada or one of the EU countries either don't speak the native language at all, or know only a little. The language barrier can get in the way of finding a job, making friends, processing paperwork, and even getting adequate medical care. But, learning a new language isn't easy. If you're reading this book, it means that, at minimum, you know English, which is great. Even if you don't speak Swedish, German, French, or Dutch, you'll be able to communicate with locals, and maybe even officials. The keyword here is 'maybe', because citizens of EU countries don't always accept communicating in English, in an effort to preserve the significance of their language. However, depending on your situation and the matter of urgency in different dealings, chances are that people will still be willing to speak to you in English.

But, how do you go about learning a country's native language?

If you head to one of the previously mentioned countries, and depending on your status and individual situation, you'll either get free language classes and be required to have a certificate of completion to be able to work, or you'll join a class or a course at your own expense. The latter rarely happens unless you choose to do so, but it's important to note that, if you can fund your education, you can choose a more advanced course that will help you land better-paid jobs, particularly if you have a college degree.

Aside from taking classes, there are other things you can do to learn any domestic language faster:

- Ask for help. Everyone likes a person who wants to learn their language. If you're shopping or running errands, ask someone who speaks English to help you learn basic words and phrases needed daily, including names of foods, drinks, paperwork, streets, how to ask for directions, how to ask which bus, train, or subway to take to get to a certain place, etc.
- Connect with people from your country living in the same community. They can be a big, if not main, source of help. They can help you to learn the domestic language, but also give town-specific tips for how to run errands, get to important locations, shop for groceries, etc. If you have a roommate who speaks the native language,

take some time during the day to speak only that language at home. Don't be ashamed of your poor grammar and clunky words. It won't take long before you know the language well enough to get by on your own, and, of course, start working.

- Work is also a great place to perfect your language skills. Similar to the USA, the vast majority of EU and Canada locals will welcome you and will want to be helpful, language skills included. Don't hesitate to ask if you're not certain, and try spending as much time speaking the domestic language as possible.
- Most immigrants and expats become fluent in foreign languages within a year of living in the country. If you come across any problems with language-learning, you can always ask your appointed caretakers (e.g. social works, therapists, doctors) for help, and they'll help you sign up for extra classes.

Adapting to New Cultures

Coming to Western society from an Asian or an African country often causes a phenomenon known as 'culture shock.' Simply put, life in Western societies might be completely different than what you're used to. While a promise of job opportunities, quality education, and an overall better quality life make many European countries an immigrant-friendly environment, getting used to these new environments is a big change, and there's no shame in it. If you move to one of the countries listed above, those you come across (healthcare workers, policemen, teachers, and fellow citizens) will understand that you're going through a major change.

Everything will be strange when you arrive on new soil. Landscapes, weather, food, and unknown languages can make you feel out of place. On top of that, different customs, values, and fashion also take time to get used to. How big of a change it will be for you depends on how familiar you are with Western culture, whether or not you've traveled or studied abroad, and of course, the type of environment you come from.

People who migrate to different countries can experience depression, fatigue, irritability, frustration, and can generally start feeling out of place.

The common three stages of culture shock include (Ward, et al. 2001):

- **The honeymoon stage.** After you've reached new lands where you feel safe and are given opportunities to prosper, you'll enjoy rooting into your new environment. Your family will most likely be safe and taken care of for the first time in a long time, and you won't worry about food or healthcare. You'll enjoy furnishing your place of living and doing paperwork to start looking for a job. This is a great change compared to past struggles, and you might feel like nothing can ruin your happiness.
- **Rejection**. Things can get a bit trickier when you start actively participating in the community. You'll start to realize that the language barrier makes life more challenging than you assumed, and you can encounter hostile behaviors and racism. There's also a possibility that highly liberal Western societies make for an awkward daily experience, as you'll start feeling like much of what happens conflicts with your values and beliefs. It's important to keep in mind that Western European societies emphasize social equality for all. That means that you, as well as others around you, have the right to live according to their culture and values.
- **Recovery**. After some time, you'll start making friends and connections one way or another. You'll find a way to fit into the environment while honoring your own culture and values, and feel more like you belong. The better you learn the country's language, the more you'll be able to communicate with people around you, and you'll learn plenty of new and useful things about your town.

Adopting a Different Lifestyle

Culture shock is normal for everyone who changes countries and cultures, and it's not specific to you. It's important to acknowledge that it will take the time to get used to a new environment, meaning that you should keep a journal, stay in touch with friends and family, and find locals who are willing to talk about cultural differences with you. At the end of the day, adaptation is all about finding your happy medium between the new habits you want to adopt, and the old ones you want to keep. Keep in mind that Canada, Australia, and EU countries encourage immigrants to maintain and nurture their culture, and there will probably be at least one organization in your town centered around your native culture. Connect with these organizations, and you'll feel a lot less homesick. Here's a shortlist for what you can do to manage easier in a new environment:

- Find out what an average routine looks like. Where should you go to get groceries, when, and how (transportation)? What time does the workday usually start, when's the best time to head to work, what's the best time to cook and clean, when do you socialize? Of course, all of these are yours to decide, but common daily routines are often linked with work hours, transportation, closing times for shops and public venues like parks, restaurants, and coffee shops.
- Know what paperwork you should have with you on all times and occasions
- Know when and how to get to places you need on a daily basis (e.g. bank, post office, doctor's, etc.)

- Make sure you have emergency phone numbers, and know what to say in case you need urgent assistance (e.g. medical, police, firefighters, etc.)
- What degree of formality is required for different occasions (work, free time, beach, going out, etc.). You're, of course, free to wear the clothing you wish, particularly if your outfits have a religious or cultural significance. However, some occasions require being more formal, and some less, which really depends on individual and cultural circumstances.

Chapter 5: Leave and Let go

When to Abandon Your Current Residence

But, what happens if you don't adapt well to the new environment, or aren't treated as fairly as you'd expect? There are things that could make an environment hostile for you regardless of the government's immigration policies. They include:

- Harsh climate that negatively affects your health: Many of the recommended countries have quite different climates than you might be used to. Some are extremely hot, like Australia, or can get extremely cold, like Canada, Sweden, or Finland. Continental climate present in Germany, Netherlands, and Italy can get quite humid and rainy, which may not work well if you have respiratory issues. If any of the environmental factors are affecting your health, you should think about moving.

- Local unemployment: Employment opportunities aren't the same across the board, and you could end up in a town where it's hard to get a job. In that case, you should think about relocating.
- Hostile environment: Racism and bigotry are commonly present in all populations to a certain degree. It's always possible to end up in a town where diversity isn't appreciated, in which case you should consider moving to a more accepting area.
- Legal unfairness and bad treatment by authorities: Regardless of a country's official policies, it's always possible to end up in a town that doesn't value cultural and racial diversity and legal and social equality. If you've been continuously treated unfairly based on race and ethnicity, and the response to your reports hasn't been satisfactory, you should consider relocating to a more accepting environment.

Mental and Health Benefits From Finding The Right Environment

Being in a toxic environment, where you're exposed to constant stress, fear, and discrimination, can have negative effects on your health. Self-esteem, as well as physical health, can suffer the longer you suffer discrimination. Stress, depression, cardiovascular problems, and other health issues that may arise if you haven't been getting adequate medical care, should soon subside if you find the right environment.

If you've already had negative experiences as a non-native in a particular country and you feel like it damages your health, you should ask one of your appointed caregivers to help you settle in a different town. They should be able to help you find a friendlier environment, and also explore job opportunities.

You should ask for medical and psychological help if you think that your health has diminished. Once you start living in a more friendly environment, you should start sleeping better, feeling less anxious and stressed, and if you had any psychosomatic symptoms due to stress (e.g. high blood pressure, migraine, loss of appetite), they should subside as well.

Conclusion

The goal of this book was to point out some of the major concerns related to migration and seeking asylum in the USA, as well to show that there are plenty of alternatives. In this book, you first learned that US immigration policies started becoming more hostile since 2016, when Donald Trump was elected. You learned that there are many recorded cases of police brutality, unequal treatment, and human rights violations committed by US authorities in regards to immigrants, refugees, and asylum-seekers. You learned that the social situation in the US isn't favorable as well, with demonstrations and protests due to police brutality receiving little to no response from the government.

All of this goes to show that the US, for the time being, may not be the best place for you. On the bright side, as you learned, there are plenty of other countries that welcome newcomers and have pretty well-organized support programs. Canada, Australia, Sweden, Finland, Germany, Netherlands, Italy, Denmark, Spain, and France, are among the countries that are known for their pro-immigration policies. These countries are the places to expect a humane, fair treatment at the very least, and proper education, housing, and employment if you become a permanent immigrant.

As you learned in this book, things don't always get easier even once you do find a friendly country to live in. Language barriers and culture shock occur for the majority of people who change countries, and finding yourself homesick and depressed is to be expected when you're facing a completely different culture and lifestyle. But, as you learned, most people adapt over time. You too will find ways to fit into the basic lifestyle and routine of your new country while maintaining your culture, language, individuality, and customs.

You also learned that finding a good environment may not always be easy. It's always possible for extreme weather to cause health complications, and of course, individual towns don't necessarily align with national policies when it comes to immigration. Acceptance and tolerance isn't even across the board, and if you find yourself chronically stressed and constantly facing rasism, discrimination, and unfair treatment, the best thing to do is look for a more accepting place to live. As you learned, being discriminated against can cause a lot of stress, and even anxiousness and depression. This can diminish your physical health, causing chronic pains, cardiovascular problems, and further health issues. But, as you learned, finding a good environment to live in should help you recover both physically and mentally.

Many people move to multiple cities and change countries multiple times to find the right place to settle, and you shouldn't feel ashamed to leave an environment that's not working out for you for any reason. The best way to find out which place is best for you is to consult with organizations that help immigrants, and find out which countries and towns best align with your personality and expertise. Good luck on your journey!

References

Canada court rules US "unsafe" for asylum seekers. (2020, July 22). BBC News. https://www.bbc.com/news/world-us-canada-53494561

Human rights office decries disproportionate use of force in US protests. (2020, July 24). UN News. https://news.un.org/en/story/2020/07/1068971

Jones, J. M. (2019, February 20). *Americans less satisfied with treatment of minority groups*. Gallup.Com; Gallup. https://news.gallup.com/poll/246866/americans-less-satisfied-treatment-minority-groups.aspx

Krogstad, J. M. (2020, June 17). *Americans broadly support legal status for immigrants brought to the U.S. illegally as children*. Pew Research Center. https://www.pewresearch.org/fact-tank/2020/06/17/americans-broadly-support-legal-status-for-immigrants-brought-to-the-u-s-illegally-as-children/

Packer, S. G. (2020, April.). *The president is winning his war on american institutions*. The Atlantic. https://www.theatlantic.com/magazine/archive/2020/04/how-to-destroy-a-government/606793/

The 80 best countries for immigrants. (2019). Usnews.Com. https://www.usnews.com/news/best-countries/best-immigrants

Ward, C. A., Bochner, S., & Furnham, A. (2001). *The psychology of culture shock*. Psychology Press.